STITCH YOUR TORN DREAMS

10 WAYS TO DISCOVER YOUR TRUTH & REBUILD

ARYAMBA SN

Chennai • Bangalore

CLEVER FOX PUBLISHING
Chennai, India

Published by CLEVER FOX PUBLISHING 2025
Copyright © Aryamba SN 2025

All Rights Reserved.
ISBN: 978-93-67078-90-7

This book has been published with all reasonable efforts taken to make the material error-free after the consent of the author. No part of this book shall be used, reproduced in any manner whatsoever without written permission from the author, except in the case of brief quotations embodied in critical articles and reviews.

The Author of this book is solely responsible and liable for its content including but not limited to the views, representations, descriptions, statements, information, opinions and references ["Content"]. The Content of this book shall not constitute or be construed or deemed to reflect the opinion or expression of the Publisher or Editor. Neither the Publisher nor Editor endorse or approve the Content of this book or guarantee the reliability, accuracy or completeness of the Content published herein and do not make any representations or warranties of any kind, express or implied, including but not limited to the implied warranties of merchantability, fitness for a particular purpose. The Publisher and Editor shall not be liable whatsoever for any errors, omissions, whether such errors or omissions result from negligence, accident, or any other cause or claims for loss or damages of any kind, including without limitation, indirect or consequential loss or damage arising out of use, inability to use, or about the reliability, accuracy or sufficiency of the information contained in this book.

CONTENTS

About the Author .... *v*
Acknowledgements .... *vii*
Preface .... *ix*

1. Weaving Two Lives Together 1
2. The Birth of a Mother 13
3. The Birth of a Mother: Season 2 18
4. Loss and Redirection 34
5. Health is Wealth 42
6. Stepping Into Confidence: a Walk That Changed Things 49
7. Giving Back: Purpose Through Service 58
8. Finding My Voice 66
9. Loss of An Anchor and Life-Long Learning 74
10. Stitching the Tapestry of My Life 80

ABOUT THE AUTHOR

*A*ryamba SN, a Master in Computer Application, believes that life's second innings can be more vibrant than the first. After a significant pause in her corporate career to embrace motherhood, she emerged as a multi-faceted achiever, proving that self-reinvention knows no boundaries.

Her literary journey includes co-authoring "Inked Imagination" and "Strings Attached," while her editorial expertise shines through her compilation work in "Strings Attached" and as editor of "The Scarecrow Chronicles." These works reflect her dedication to bringing diverse voices to the forefront of literature. Her writing portfolio extends to profile writings in B'youtiful magazine and articles in the Mumbai Global Newspaper. SOT publications recognised her contributions in writing with the Inquill Holders' Award. Her inspiring transformation journey caught the attention of Femina magazine, which featured her achievements.

Currently serving as the Maharashtra President of the Women's Chamber of Commerce and Industry (WICCI) Equality and Empowerment wing, she channels her experience into creating opportunities for women's

ABOUT THE AUTHOR

advancement. As a coordinator at Robinhood Academy, she continues to foster educational empowerment in her community. In a compelling interview with the COEP Blog Team titled "Empowering Voices: A Deep Dive into Feminism and Equality," she shares her insights on women's empowerment and the evolving landscape of gender equality in modern India.

She was crowned Mrs Elixir India in the sports category in 2020 and won the Mrs. Swag Icon of India in 2021. She is also a receiver of the Pune Diva Award. She has done shoots for magazines and a calendar. She demonstrates that age is no barrier to pursuing new passions. An ex-employee of Amazon and alumnus of IIT Roorkee's Data Science and AI program, she continues to embrace learning and growth.

Through her journey from homemaker to author, athlete, and data scientist, she exemplifies the power of knowing oneself and becoming more. Her story continues to inspire others to stitch their torn dreams into beautiful realities.

ACKNOWLEDGEMENTS

*I*n the tapestry of life, each thread represents someone who has shaped our journey. My deepest gratitude begins with my parents, who planted my heart's first seeds of dreams. To my father, who taught me that courage wears many faces, and my mother, who showed me what love and kindness are and whose presence continues to guide me even in their absence—your love remains my foundation.

To my husband, my steadfast partner in the dance of life—thank you for holding space for my dreams while helping me to keep my feet on the ground. Your belief in me has been my anchor through every storm and celebration. To my children, my most excellent teachers: you've shown me that love grows when shared and that it's never too late to chase rainbows. Your understanding during my journey of self-discovery has been my greatest gift.

To my siblings, my first friends and eternal cheerleaders—thank you for keeping me grounded while encouraging me to soar. Your laughter, wisdom, and unwavering support have been my constant companions.

ACKNOWLEDGEMENTS

To my parents-in-law: thank you for embracing me as your own and creating a home where dreams are nurtured.

Life has blessed me with extraordinary companions—my friends who have celebrated me throughout, fellow dreamers who taught me persistence, communities that showed me balance, and kindred spirits who proved every milestone possible. To all who journeyed alongside me and helped me rediscover my sparkle—you've made this adventure meaningful. To my corporate colleagues who welcomed me back to the professional world with open arms—your support has been invaluable. To my editors, mentors, and everyone who has touched this journey with their wisdom and kindness, you've each added a unique hue to my story's palette.

Finally, to every dreamer who picks up this book, thank you for allowing me to share this journey with you. May you find the courage to turn your dreams into reality.

PREFACE

When I began writing this book, I had a straight forward question: Can our torn dreams truly be mended? The answer revealed itself through my transformation journey—not just mended but rewoven into something far more magnificent than initially imagined.

My qualifications for writing this book don't come from academic degrees in psychology or life coaching. They come from living the journey this book describes—from stepping away from a corporate career to embrace motherhood to returning to the professional world after a fourteen-year gap. Each role I've inhabited—parent, professional, athlete, writer, and pageant winner—has contributed unique threads to this tapestry of understanding.

This book's research spans personal experience and extensive interviews with individuals who have successfully navigated their paths of reinvention. What began as a personal journal of self-discovery evolved into a structured guide as I noticed common patterns in successful transformations—whether you're changing careers, processing loss, or simply seeking more meaning in life.

PREFACE

It is not another self-help book. What makes this different? The uniqueness lies in its approach to self-knowledge as the foundation of transformation. Rather than offering quick fixes or one-size-fits-all solutions, this book guides you through personal archaeology—helping you uncover your authentic self and build from there.

New neuroscience research has further validated what I discovered through experience: self-awareness and intentional action can rewire our brains, creating new pathways for success at any age. This book integrates these insights while remaining grounded in practical, accessible strategies.

In case you are wondering if it's too late to change, your dreams are too torn to repair, or you are selfish for wanting more, this book holds the answers for you. It's not about starting over; it's about starting from where you are with all the wisdom you've gained.

Let's begin this journey of knowing, becoming, and rebuilding—together.

CHAPTER 1
WEAVING TWO LIVES TOGETHER

*"I know that your soul fails to find a voice.
Instead, it uncovers through your eyes, a gaze of
unsaid words, intense, sharp, that swirls my soul.
I know, you fret the storm I sense, by your gaze
of unsaid words"*

That March evening, my nerves were on edge, and all I could think about was avoiding the embarrassment of sweat dripping down my face. About 700 well-dressed people, murmuring with jolly expressions, looked furtively at us, the newlyweds. They were even more shy than we were when they looked at us. Some children looked at us and dreamed of their big day, and elderly couples reminisced about their wedding day and the journey. We had to register our marriage during the four days of the wedding. The mangalsutra was still foreign to me, and bangles jingled every moment. I wore a heavy Kancheevaram silk sari with jasmine strings tied to my hair when I went with my husband, Rajesh, and father to register our marriage. A man sitting in an office chair at the registry office said, "Would it be better if we delete your father's name and add your husband's"?

I found him inconsiderate and felt very distressed—a difficult decision. I looked at my father, who had given me an identity and a life, and my husband, who would become my everything. I was alone in this struggle to choose. I marvelled at the clarity of my husband's life: that he never needed to change his name. His identity was like a pillar that stood unshakable, untouched. I did not dare to cut my father's name from myself and asked the office person to retain my maiden name. My husband, oblivious to the storm inside me, smiled and seemed proud of my decision. I heard my father saying, "What's in the name"? I still have my maiden name, and I'm proud of it. Yet, I feel powerless in the absence of my mother's name in my name, though she is such an integral part of my existence.

I was in the middle of a project in ABB and could not fly with Rajesh after the ceremony.

I joined him after six months in a new country. While thrilled about my new life, I experienced moments of anxiety as I had to navigate the unfamiliarity of marriage.

I learned to communicate as open and honest communication becomes paramount, addressing concerns, expressing needs and actively listening to the partner. As a newlywed girl, I was eager to explore new hobbies with my partner and discover shared passions and interests that could enrich our lives. Finding the right balance between maintaining my interests and hobbies while fully embracing my role as a wife was made easy by my open, adjusting and loving husband. He showed empathy, which I badly needed to adapt to the new house, city, country and person.

As the days passed, we learnt the art of building intimacy, physical and emotional. The days were filled with intense love, where every moment spent with him felt like a precious memory, filled with stolen glances, playful banter, and a deep sense of connection. I started to learn to read his silence after a tough day at work, and he understood when I needed a hug more than solutions. We had many beautiful evenings where we both sat on the balcony of a sprawling house, sharing dreams we had never told anyone else. One's hand reached for another's naturally, without thinking, and realized it had become our reflex, and it continues till now. I remember the comfortable silences that grew between conversations, no longer needing to fill every moment with words. We had most of the evenings spent together with music. Rajesh introduced me to country music, Lobo, Kenny Rogers, Jorge Jones and John Denver. I introduced him to Backstreet Boys, Boyzone, MLTR, George Micheal, and Michael Jackson. He introduced me to spiritual books and discourses. I have been brought up by parents for whom spirituality was the way of life, and my husband's place is where I started reading many books in the genre. I saw him as a voracious reader who welcomed me into a world of music, love, books and dining.

I was energetic, intuitive and spontaneous, and he was analytical and methodical. I quickly embraced new ideas, and he evaluated them before taking action. I was emotionally expressive, and he was emotionally steady. I was an adrenaline junkie, and he was calm, tranquil, slow and quiet. My spontaneous decisions, my enthusiasm for trying new things, and my need for a lot of conversation over dinner sometimes used to get doused off, anticipating his stresses and understanding his silences. But also, how it sometimes made me take things personally. I was disappointed when there was no one left to tango with.

The truth I did not understand then was that my expressive nature complemented his calm stability. He listened and offered a structured perspective as I spiralled through my thoughts aloud. His consistency maintained my flights of fantasy without clipping their wings. When making decisions, I brought possibilities, but he brought practicality. My fervour lit his careful track, and his tenacity supported my lofty dreams. Together, we have created something neither of us could have accomplished alone.

However, through these challenges, a beautiful transformation began to unfold for me. I started evolving with Rajesh and his demeanour. Eventually, I started working as a system analyst in a computer service company and later was a Computer Science lecturer for BSC students till we decided to have a kid and give more meaning to our relationship.

Marriage and Torn Dreams in Relationships

Losing identity is a profound challenge, particularly when transitioning to a new environment. Marriage signified a change in relationship status and a significant shift in lifestyle and location. I sometimes felt isolated and at a loss. Friends and family members who once extended the security net were miles away, leaving me lonely and disconnected.

My reflection in the mirror of my wedding dress on the wedding day perfectly represented our life together. Various colours and patterns of reality were visible. I dreamt of fairy tales in marriage – flawless comprehension, unrelenting affection, and effortless adjustments. My dreams appeared to break down when my creative chaos and Rajesh's analytical calm were exposed in reality, and spontaneous planning clashed with methodical thinking. His silence, logic, and unpassionate approach made every minor disappointment a perfect imperfection – whether I wanted to express myself or seek an emotional connection.

Every moment was different. I was struggling to reconcile our differences with a sense of expectation.

I acknowledged the differences in empowering myself to reclaim my identity while embracing my new role. During my journey from failure to revelation, I discovered that crushed hopes occasionally yield more robust answers. The change began when I stopped seeing our differences as cracks in the dream and started seeing them as unique patterns in a new design.

Stitch Your Torn Dreams:

To stitch your dreams together, you must acknowledge the torn dream, discover your truth, and then rebuild it.

1. **Acknowledge**: You need to acknowledge that you have issues. To accept and understand the reality of shattered dreams, you need to recognise your emotions, accept the current situation without judgment, and reframe your perspective to see potential learning opportunities and new paths forward, allowing yourself to grieve the loss of the dream while recognizing that it doesn't define your future and can lead to positive growth.
2. **Discover your truth**: To know your truth in marriage, answer these questions:

- Do you expect a perfect spouse?

Great marriages are not made by having the perfect spouse. Show grace for imperfections. Instead, a great marriage happens when two people are reasonably compatible; each looks for the good in the other and supports, forgives and respects the other.

- Do you expect your spouse to fill your life?

Many couples have unrealistic expectations that their marriage will help "fill" or "repair" the broken parts of their lives. It happens to some extent, but not entirely. Your marriage is more powerful when you have multiple friends, family, and interests in your life.

- Are you a passive partner?

You get out of your marriage what you put into it. If you invest time, thought, and energy into building a stronger, healthier relationship, you will likely have a great one.

- Have you invested?

Marriage is like an investment account. The more you invest in building a strong connection with your spouse (showing kindness, support, affection, and respect), the larger your emotional bank account will be. That way, if you miss the mark sometimes, you will have enough "emotional resources" to make up for the loss your relationship will suffer.

- Is love a verb or a noun for you?

Realize that love is about more than just emotions and feelings. At its core, love is a commitment to do what's best for the other person, and this commitment must be expressed in daily actions that are supportive, affirming, and respectful.

3. **Rebuild the dreams:** Without acknowledging and knowing your truth, you cannot rebuild your dreams.

Ten ways to rebuild your dreams in marriage

1. **Commit**: Pledging to the cause is crucial before you make an effort. Actions are based upon intentions; thus, for rebuilding a marriage, first, what you intend to do should be made clear, especially to yourself. It would help if you were clear about what you hope to work on and want to put in the work to rebuild a marriage. Knowing your goals enables you to create a path to achieve them. Your heart needs to be invested in rebuilding what you lost.

2. **Remove the obstacles**: Determining what hinders your path to a happy marriage is another critical aspect. Such obstacles occur because sometimes, you might have failed in at least one of these four deterrents necessary in rebuilding your marriage: not forgiving, unfriendly interactions, untrustworthiness, and the doubt of having your trust broken again (feeling betrayed). So, focus on eliminating those hurdles to build the foundation of a blissful married life. Don't hesitate to converse with your spouse about such issues.

3. **Explore what brings happiness and satisfaction in the relationship.** Three things make every relationship joyful.
   - love
   - trust
   - open communications

   The things that make a person happy and satisfied in a relationship are personal. For instance, how you describe bliss and fulfilment in a marriage may differ concerning your spouse. Things that make you feel loved may not be the same things that make your spouse feel loved. Accept this concept and rediscover what relationship joy means to you and your significant other. Try to know what you both want and then use that knowledge to strengthen your bond.

4. **Adjust your demands**: Marriages experience issues and clashes. Some marital problems and conflicts can be expected and be kept away. Others can't be predicted and should be managed in time to save the relationship. Rebuilding broken dreams in marriage requires efforts from both. Resolving conflicts together can deepen appreciation in a relationship, enabling couples to grow and achieve greater mutual fulfilment in their marriage.

5. **Emphasize changing yourself, not your partner**: Insisting your mate to live according to your

specifications doesn't always work. In the first place, you can't transform another person. You can change yourself. Attempting to mould your mate will pressure your relationship and debilitate them from evolving. Regardless of whether your mate does change, they won't feel great about the relationship until you accept changing for them. If nagging your spouse to change deteriorates your marriage, rebuild the relationship. It's pivotal to acknowledge responsibility for your mistakes instead of accusing your spouse. Start with bringing a positive change in yourself before expecting it from your spouse.

6. **Take guidance from the third person**: Though it becomes unacceptable to live your married life with interference from a third person, sometimes, asking for advice and help from your loyal friends and family members becomes crucial. Experienced married couples can help you out with specific issues. Depending on your troubles, you can also seek marriage counselling.

7. **Fulfil your partner's emotional needs**: To rebuild your marriage, it's essential to be committed to each other's needs, whether physical, financial, or emotional. Everyone has a different perspective regarding love. Sharing emotions, being valued, spending time together, working on your friendship,

and sharing experiences are examples of strengthening a marriage.

8. **Be clear about what you want from your marriage**: As every couple is different, so is marriage. You need to know what you want from the marriage before you understand how to rebuild a marriage. Some couples want to share visions, life goals, and expectations. Some couples like to lead an individual life and connect in a less dependent way. The dynamics here rely entirely on the individuals. The bottom line is knowing what you want from a marriage; you might be looking for something else, and your partner might want something else. It would help if you had a detailed conversation about it.

9. **Be friends**: The best way to rebuild a marriage is to start from the basics. If you think it's too much for both of you to be romantically involved right now. Try maintaining a healthy friendship. It is said that couples with strong friendships are more likely to be happy with each other. Try to build a friendly bond with each other first, and then figure out how you want to work on your marriage. Talk to each other about dreams, hopes and goals. Make sure that you both are honest and respect each other. Accepting the differences and working towards a better future will make things easy.

10. **Ask for professional help**: If nothing works when rebuilding a marriage, seek professional help. Visit a marriage counsellor or a psychotherapist. Someone experienced can explain why you cannot revive the attachment in your relationship. Depending on your issues and disagreements, they can give you better and more personalised advice. Try to be as honest as you can be with your therapist, as you can only rebuild a marriage when you identify the root cause of the problem.

CHAPTER 2
FOURTEEN YEARS OF PAUSE: THE BIRTH OF A MOTHER

*M*y life's centre of gravity started shifting along with my body's. I was carrying my first child in me. I went through severe morning sickness for three months. Imagine a person continuously puking at a hat's drop for three months. I lived on half an apple daily for three months. I doubted my existence, let alone eating.

Somehow, things got easier after 3 months. I could enjoy the rest of my pregnancy. I cared for my physical, emotional and mental well-being for the rest of the trimesters. I never had community support as we were out of India. It is not the only baby that grows inside her; a Mother's Faculty sprouts and roots itself during pregnancy. Resilience, strength, intuitions, quick responses, giving, caring, fighting spirit, selflessness and other things make up this faculty. It is different from the earlier one. This faculty lies dormant in a pregnant woman since the baby needs to nourish it.

When I saw my baby, I felt like I was seeing someone else's baby and could not believe I finally became a mom. A sweet, tiny, beautiful bundle sleeping beside me was like a dream. She was very pretty. The Mother's Faculty does not surface soon after the baby is born. The birth of a mother does not take place in one dramatic, defining moment. I was naive about holding, feeding, and caring for the newborn. Society, including the hospital staff, expected me to be an ace at it, a superwoman and supermom, to be specific and cater to the new bundle's needs with drips and catheters plugged into me. How senseless the people make of themselves. When a mother is born, she should not err, rest, or think for herself.

I needed time to come out of the drugs and sedation I was administered- to fathom what had happened in my life. I tried to take some time to make sense of the situation between the pouring visitors. It was a new journey for me and my baby to get to know each other.

For many more months, days and nights merged into a whirly period of rocking, feeding, diaper change, snuggling, and, if possible, napping every twenty-four hours. I had developed a new repertoire of feelings and behaviours, utterly different from the pre-baby period.

The Mother's faculty also started developing as my baby started nourishing it.

The Mother's faculty determines what we consider most important, how quickly we respond, how adaptable we are to unpredicted events, what we are sensitive to, and what we notice in a given situation. It dictates what we find pleasant and exciting, frightening or tedious. A woman's life fundamentally changes with the baby's arrival, and she enters the realm of experience unknown to others and herself.

It was daunting to suddenly hold myself responsible for another life. The absolute accountability was of another magnitude entirely. I did not fear it but did not take it lightly. Every day, I gathered strength from Mother's Faculty and the baby, for whom I was the Universe. I gradually gained the confidence and assurance needed when I saw my baby flourishing.

When a daughter becomes a mother, her outlook on her mother changes. She starts looking at her mother entirely through a different lens. Motherhood is unique to each woman and is shared by all mothers. I needed to connect with mothers to get that cushioning, and I needed a community where I was understood, cared for, loved, and not judged. I included my mother, mother-in-law, sisters, and friends in the community. Motherhood is a lonely place. Though you are with an understanding, supportive family, a mother needs her community.

Those were not Google, Instagram, Facebook, ChatGPT, or Netflix days. If someone needed to find something, it used to be books, making a beeline to the resource, or digging deep inside your being. One man who came to my rescue during my pregnancy and child-rearing phase was Dr. Spock. From information about how an embryo starts getting limbs and a heart-beat, what a baby looks like at a specific month in the uterus, what you need to do and how to be as an expecting mother, how you should welcome a newborn, how to fulfil its expectations in the new environment, when and how to introduce solids, when and how to wean her off from Mother's milk, how to pacify her when she had colic, ways to read to a three-month-old baby, how to trick the baby and the ways to win as a parent, etc., to every psychological need of the baby explained in the book written by Dr Spock. The book was my saviour. It had become my Bhagavad-Gita ever since I conceived. It still occupies a space in my bookshelf. I owe to Dr Spock in this lifetime for hand-holding me during the pregnancy, childbirth, child rearing and beyond. It laid a strong foundation for parenting and also the art of parenting in me. The courses I did and the workshops I underwent about parenting later in life are additional layers to his rock-solid core insights.

My baby started walking around the house, talking gibberish and playing with toys. She always listened to the stories I read and enjoyed the colourful illustrations in the book. She was a happy baby, and watching her grow was a delight.

We relocated to another country with my one-and-a-half-year-old daughter.

CHAPTER 3
THE BIRTH OF A MOTHER: SEASON 2

*T*ransitioning to a new country with a toddler was challenging. We needed to adapt to the new milieu. We needed to relocate to Indonesia. The process of integrating into new communities took time for me. Another substantial barrier was the language barrier. I needed to learn Bahasa Indonesia. It was not easy to connect with locals. Again, there was no Google translator or voice-to-text AI tool then. I had to take the help of a book – English to Bahasa language translator. Establishing an aid network in a new nation proved to be demanding. It took time for me to form new friendships, and I often found myself surrounded by unfamiliar individuals. A lack of strong support networks made adjusting harder for me and my toddler. I accessed the Mother's faculty in me to find ways to comfort my child while also handling my own emotions.

I soon found that my daughter was adapting to the new country well, learning a new language, and attending preschool when she turned three.

I always wanted two children, and we were adding one more member to our family.

I experienced mixed emotions when I became pregnant with my second child. Along with the excitement of having a new baby, I felt more confident in my ability to provide for my children. The second pregnancy differed positively from the first as I knew about the journey ahead. I knew the challenges – feeding, sleep, continuous vigil over the child. I was better prepared for the second one. Moreover, the relationship with the first child had modified my perspectives towards pregnancy and parenting. My special affection for the journey allowed me to experience and embrace the challenges of raising a family. I was grateful for the unique perspective. I was thankful for the book from Dr. Spock.

The second baby arrived, and everything changed for us as a family. I no longer needed to entertain and keep my daughter occupied as she got busy knowing her brother. My second baby accepted the outer world well and fast. We felt complete with his arrival. We shifted to India with an infant. Again, we had to realign our lives with two kids in the family. It proved more manageable for me to run the house, kids, and family in other countries than in India, as

I had never done that in India. After I got married, I was in different countries with full-time professional house help staying with us. The real struggle started brewing when we returned and had no professional house help. Those were the days with no structured agencies for nannies and professionals. I wasted no energy finding one, deciding to manage the kids alone.

I was growing up as a mother with my children. A mother was born and was growing. I was also getting into the zone of Maternal conflicts.

The Silent Struggle: Maternal Conflicts

It is a common belief that motherhood is a pure and enjoyable experience. Nonetheless, it's pretty intricate. The emotions experienced by mothers can vary greatly, ranging from love hearts and joy hearts to frustrations and exhaustion or resentment. A mother's conflicting thoughts can be a complex combination of love, duty and fear. While mothers significantly impact their kids' lives, the demands of being occupied with children can also be emotionally draining. It is the juxtaposition of opposing feelings, and it's part of Mum's guilt but not out of herself. A mother's love for her children is so great that it makes all those things more important than anything else. This act of selflessness is admirable but can also be a source of guilt. Mothers face the challenge of balancing family life and personal ambitions. While a mother may desire to pursue her career or hobbies, she must also acknowledge the emotional strain of leaving her children behind.

I had an opportunity to teach in an academy where I needed to prepare executives for post-graduation in software skills. The duration of coaching was in the morning, three hours from 6 am, and in the evening, four hours from 6 pm since it was for working executives. My first reaction was like a free person who would conquer the world with the presented opportunity. I was elated. It came after a break of six years. My younger one was one year old, and my elder was five. Eventually, I had to drop it as those were the crucial hours my family needed me, my husband attending the office, and a kid attending school. I had to put it on the back burner as I decided to give my best to the kids and the family. I was indispensable to the family.

I appreciate women with the capacity and strength to manage both sides. I knew myself sufficiently that I could not multitask.

Two opposing emotions were simultaneously present. Motherhood means loving your kids deeply while not being able to enjoy certain aspects, such as lack of sleep or loss of personal freedom. These opposing emotions can be confusing. While the transition to motherhood is enjoyable, it can also be physically and mentally draining. The constant responsibility of childcare can result in motherhood responsibilities that can lead to emotional distress, exhaustion, loss of loved ones, and even bitterness. The needs of the mother and the baby often overlay, so it can be challenging to balance. The idea of a flawless mother is a myth. When a mother doesn't meet these expectations, she may feel overwhelmed and inadequate, leading to stress and self-doubt. This fits into the ambiguity surrounding success and failure in parenting. Managing these feelings without guilt or shame can be accomplished by admitting them as an inherent aspect of motherhood rather than a reflection of one's worthiness.

Mothers' contested ideas are born from love, social pressures, personal goals, and family dynamics. Understanding her internal obstacles and offering her empathy can boost her well-being.

Opportunities for Growth

Acknowledging Maternal conflicts can lead to personal development. They are not something to turn down, and they can stimulate creativity in caregiving. If a mother is stressed from not having enough time to be alone, she can be flexible and find new ways to make time for herself. She can be creative and adaptable to changing situations. She navigates a beautiful spectrum of emotions, and this complexity is natural! Accepting, embracing, and understanding them helps her find strength and connection in the journey. By doing so, the journey to know oneself as a mother starts. Once one knows herself, she can avoid falling into unhealthy coping patterns that may arise during difficult times. Maternal conflicts impact the mother and the child. Research indicates that mothers who are open about their ambivalent feelings may have a greater sense of control regarding parenting. However, failing to acknowledge these feelings may lead to dysfunctional tendencies like irritability and emotional withdrawal.

The Tight Bubble of Total Focus

After I had kids, I forgot who I was before, what I wanted to do in life, what I wanted to buy, what I wanted to eat, and how to invest time in getting prepared for any wedding or any event. Seeing the morning sun first every day, day after day, did not fetch me any price. I made lunch boxes for three, got the kids ready for school at different times, and dropped the first at the bus stop to see the second one waiting for me to get him ready. Running the house errands till I fetch them back one after the other at different times, checking their homework, planning for their extracurricular activities and meals, and many more filled my days. The same repeated for years, almost for ten years.

Since I did not have any support system like a sister or mother nearby and my husband's job involved extensive travelling, I took up my role very seriously, and why shouldn't one? A child's development and growth are greatly supported and influenced by its mother. A mother's role in her child's life is essential to promote healthy development. Of course, every mother begins to do things for her child's well-being before birth. This sacrificial but fulfilling role is not without its challenges. It was the same story with many women; I was no exception.

My existence had only one goal: My kids. Like how I took the support of Dr Spock's book in the early stages of pregnancy and infants, I needed one handholding in the later stages. I enrolled in the Infant Siddha Programme, which opened my eyes to positive parenting and introduced me to the concept of formative years. Thanks to my sister, who directed me to the course. My focus was to be there with them in their formative years. The formative years of childhood are the first eight years of a child's life and are a time of rapid development in many areas. Brain development, learning, patterns, personality, cognitive, social, emotional and physical development: These areas of development are critical during the formative years. Early childhood experiences shape a child's personality and future growth.

Children need a supportive environment and careful attention during their growing years. Positive factors that promote healthy development include stable and understanding relationships with parents and other adults, a safe and supportive environment, adequate nutrition, and social interaction. Milestones that children who have a strong foundation in their formative years form a lifelong physical and mental health and well-being.

I used to apply everything I learned from the programme at home with the kids, and they got me results. Reading to my kids started early, like when they were three months old, and it continued for a long time. This activity gave me immense pleasure as they were receptive to it. Feeding them nutritious meals was challenging as they were born with different taste buds. My entire day used to be spent strategizing how to feed and inspire them to study, finish homework, and manage extra activities. And the strategies needed customization for each kid. I used to squeeze in reading time with the younger one while at the badminton court for the elder. I never had the time and energy to think about myself, and socialization was on the back burner. Kids and their school drove my life.

I put my entire being into force to help guide me through parenting. I did everything it took, undistracted, to raise my kids. At the same time, I marvelled at other women who were doing it all, along with their professions.

Story of Every Mother

Once upon a time, a small, iridescent butterfly named Lumi lived in a vibrant forest where the trees whispered secrets to the wind. Her wings, a spectacle of shimmering blues and purples, were renowned throughout the woodland. They allowed her to dance effortlessly through the air, catching the sunlight like a thousand tiny jewels. Lumi loved to explore, soaring high above the canopy, visiting the furthest corners of the forest, and sharing tales with the other creatures she met.

But one day, a storm, unlike any other, swept through the forest. The violent winds whipped through the trees, tearing at Lumi's delicate wings, and the torrential rain battered her tiny body. When the storm finally subsided, Lumi found herself stranded on a leaf, her once vibrant wings tattered and torn, the beautiful colours fading to a dull grey.

Despair filled Lumi as she realized she could no longer fly. She watched as her friends soared through the sky, their laughter echoing through the trees, and a deep ache settled in her heart. She tried to flap her damaged wings, but they only twitched weakly, unable to lift her into the air.

A wise old owl, who had witnessed Lumi's plight, gently hooted to her, "Little Lumi, your wings may be broken, but your spirit is still strong. You can find beauty in other ways".

Lumi, hesitant at first, began exploring the forest floor, noticing details she had never seen before—the intricate patterns on a spider's web, the delicate dance of ants carrying leaves, and the vibrant colours of wildflowers pushing through the soil. She discovered a new kind of joy in the small wonders of the forest and learned to appreciate the world from a different perspective.

With time, Lumi became a storyteller. She shared her experiences with the other creatures and weaved tales of the sky from her memories of flight. Her words painted vivid pictures, allowing those who could fly to see the world through her eyes.

Though she never regained her ability to fly, Lumi's spirit soared. She became a beacon of hope, reminding everyone that even when we lose something precious, we can find beauty and meaning in unexpected places. That true strength lies in embracing change and adapting to new circumstances.

***

I thought I was losing myself, constantly giving, nurturing and supporting others. I was unaware that motherhood prepared me for many more things in life. While I was continually nurturing and providing for years, the mother's faculty I spoke about earlier was getting stronger, consolidated, expanded and integrated with my being. I put Mother's faculty above everything since it encompasses all a person needs to grow, progress, and triumph.

My daughter asked me, "What dreams did you have before becoming a mother"? I stood frozen by the kitchen counter on that day. I'd spent fourteen years pursuing motherhood, and my aspirations had faded like faded photographs. However, the question made me realize that being a mother and I were not separate dreams but part of an ongoing journey.

My Story:

Having never started any classes, I had nothing to cancel. There was no beginning of a career to be had. Most of my days were spent running around the school, completing assignments, cooking flawless meals, and maintaining a clean house as I lived my life like the perfect mother; the woman inside was silent.

Stitching the Torn Dreams

Stitching the torn dreams starts with Acknowledging, knowing your truth and Rebuilding.

Acknowledge: Know that life has changed, and your dreams might not fit the same box they used to. That doesn't mean they're gone forever; they need some tweaking to fit into your new reality. And guess what? That's perfectly okay.

Discover your Truth:

1. Establish boundaries.
   Save your precious time, energy, and space. Those boundaries are vital for mamas to maintain their identity in a world that demands motherhood. Your needs should be met.
2. Seek support.
   Meet people who share your values and beliefs. Join a supportive community of mothers and receive their support.
3. It's important to remember that you are not solely a mother.
   Realize that you aren't limited to being a mom. You possess a unique combination of interests, passions and qualities. And the world needs this!
4. Gain self-awareness.
   Appreciate your thoughts, feelings, and sensations. They are the starting point for comprehending your inner world. Push yourself to follow through and meet your boundaries. Do this.
5. Feel the fear.
   Fear often holds us back. Despite your fears, finding yourself and facing them head-on is the key to discovering who you indeed are.
6. Live a valued life.
   Reject societal expectations and follow the principles that are at stake. Be yourself.

Rebuild

Ten Ways to Rebuild Your Dreams as a Mom

1. **Build your worth**: Knowing what you're good at is crucial to achieving your goals. It's just a matter of being worthy of accomplishing your dreams. Knowledge is essential for pursuing anything beyond yourself. Make sure to reflect on your worth every day. Who were you before the arrival of the kids? Who are you now? Write down your perspective, abilities, and hobbies. When you need motivation, this will help you discover yourself. Think about these questions for ten minutes every day.

2. **Start small and dream big**: Not every situation requires a solution. Start small.

   By spending 10 minutes a day in meditation, you can gradually identify patterns and insights that will assist you in returning to the state of your former self.

   Consider them as a precursor to something bigger.

3. **Acceptance**:

   Recognizing the changes in your life is crucial. Accept them. Motherhood has its inevitable challenges. Accepting reality does not entail abandoning your dreams.

4. **Accept current reality**:

   Remember that your life is changing, and you may have to step back in certain areas. When raising children, life can be hectic and chaotic. There are moments when your children require extra attention, like feeding a hungry baby, tending to an overly active toddler, or aiding in their homework. Yet, this holds for all of us in certain circumstances. Although these moments may seem endless, they are short-lived due to the length of time. You'll have more time to focus on your goals, and your children will soon be independent.

5. **Appreciate the present**: If you're present and flexible with your timing, the beauty of motherhood can be fully realized. You are not abandoning the past but instead adjusting to your new surroundings and finding a workable solution that works for you and your loved ones.

6. **Establish a time to work towards your objective**: Let's make an effort. Creating your dreams can be achieved by dedicating a certain amount of time to working on them. And guess what? Hours of free time are not essential. Start working on your goal for ten minutes daily: This is the plan. Get started today. What's the most straightforward thing you can do today? To kickstart a business, allocate ten minutes of research to your idea. To achieve a sense of inner peace and calmness, practice by looking at yourself in the mirror. To indulge in your penchant for writing, write down your feelings or start a blog.

We need to stop overthinking it and start doing what we already have.

7. **Focus on doing, not thinking**: If you overthink, your dreams will be ruined. One can easily get caught up in figuring out why something is malfunctioning. Moving away from thinking and turning to action gives momentum. The ten minutes gradually become twenty or thirty minutes. Simple actions add up, and you suddenly achieve significant progress.

8. **Be Consistent**: The key to achieving your dreams is consistency. Over time, even minor adjustments become significant. Imagine ascending a staircase during your journey. With every step, you approach the summit. It's a gradual climb, but it'll be more manageable when you take it one step at a time.

   Appreciate your progress: Applaud all of your accomplishments, even minor ones. If you start taking action now, you'll realize that you are not just dreaming about your dreams but working towards them, which is an incredible sense of empowerment. Exactly.

9. **Find Your Peers**: Whenever you're striving, it's crucial to have the encouragement of others who understand that your dreams can be realized while also supporting and providing for your family. You can connect with your closest friends or peers on

social media, such as the Inspiring Women Society Facebook group.

Having a group of people who will be there for you is crucial, offering support and encouragement when necessary, cheering you on during difficulty, and maintaining your confidence when success is assured.

10. **Communicate your dreams**: Share your feelings with others, seek an accountability partner, and take all necessary measures to make those dreams a reality. Don't be afraid to ask for help. There are instances when speaking it out loud is the most helpful way to make it happen.

Remember:

- Zero is a valid starting point
- Progress is achieved with every small step
- Your age is your strength
- It's never too late to start!!

Bottom line: Starting from scratch is not a disadvantage. It is a blank canvas. Today, as a Maharashtra president of WICCI, an author, and a beauty pageant winner, I want to say to all mothers: Your years of total dedication as a mother are not a gap to be listed on your resume. They are the foundation for everything you want to build on next.

CHAPTER 4

LOSS AND REDIRECTION

I lost my mother in 2016. I grieved for quite long. The way people take it and process it is individualistic. Some like to talk it out and get busy. But I talked less and was in denial initially, as it was unexpected. It was a year and a half since I had met her. I felt guilty about not visiting her quarterly. The loss of her, combined with thinking of my dad losing his companion, made days empty and miserable. I wrote up until here with a flow, and it is getting difficult to write about the loss of my mother. It isn't easy to express how one feels about the void. It is a soul-stirring, heart-wrenching and brain-fogging experience. I felt terrible for Rajesh and my kids, more for the kids, as Rajesh was wise enough to soak in the atmosphere, but my kids were not. My only force in life asking me to move on was my kids. I accepted the reality and processed it to the best of my ability. I wonder if anyone can ultimately come out of it in life. The loss also allowed me to reevaluate the relationships and priorities of life. The loss also made me more resilient and aware of life's fleeting moments. She remains integral to my life in all my deeds and endeavours.

I got a job at Amazon, Pune, while still grieving. I needed to start by making my resume, but I was clueless about what to fill in. I was forty years old by then. Starting a new job after fourteen years as a stay-at-home mom can bring a whole gamut of emotions: excitement, nervousness, a sense of accomplishment, anxiety about returning to work, a new outlook on life, and even guilt about not being entirely available for the kids and the family.

I wanted to try it because I didn't want to get an attested report card of my incompetence. I was happy to be in a world of hope about my capabilities instead of getting a final verdict that I was no longer relevant in the corporate world.

A quiet voice had always asked me to do more. All those years, life had centred around everyone else. I had ignored the inner voice, but it had made its presence felt throughout.

Finally, I decided to attend the interview, seeing no loss, but I would gain some experience. I prepared myself to face the report card.

I dressed professionally for the interview. I felt excited and elated to look in the mirror. For years, I had barely looked in the mirror. I looked deep in the mirror to see a woman who might walk the path of her dreams. At the same time, fear, doubt and loss of confidence spiralled through me. I gathered the strength to step out of my cosy and protected world when I saw a mother who took on the world for her family, who could swim relentlessly to weave dreams and hopes for her children, who sowed the seed of love, trust, learning, hope, courage, faith in kids. I saw a woman who dared to dream. My report card stopped scaring me. Even if I failed, I had a safe home to return to. "We win, or we learn" became my chanting till I reached an expansive building with professionals walking and chatting. I had three rounds, including technical, communication and HR rounds, to clear. I was exhausted. I drove back home with the job in my hand.

Transitioning from a full-time mom and discovering a new arena was challenging. As one of the FANG(Facebook, Amazon, Netflix, Google) companies, Amazon demanded more from its employees. The training and learning went on till midnights. Many times, I wanted to quit and go to my comfort zone. I could afford to go through it since it was work from home. Home was where I belonged, and it was where I wanted to be. I held on to the rigorous routine as I started getting recognition and won a few awards for my performances. I worked hard and reaped the results.

Remember, a mother gives her hundred percent to whatever she takes up. I bloomed in the Amazon ecosystem with inspiring teammates, leaders, and colleagues. I gained a new community and learnt extensively.

Long ago, when I drove my kids to school, I saw many skilled and elite runners on the streets. I marvelled at their effortless running and admired the liberation they felt from running. I also desired to run and experience that freedom.

Amazon led me to that path. The work pressure was intense, and I had to do something tangentially opposite to what I did at work. I started running on the treadmill every day after work. My limbs did not support me when I tried running the first day. Why would they, anyway? I had not run ever since my seventh standard, almost three decades. Gradually, I developed the agility and the muscles for it. Running on the treadmill gave me such cushioning from the day's hardships. I did it for a long time, and it became my go-to retreat for feeling good.

Once I gained confidence in running on the treadmill, I joined the same elite runners' group at which I had looked in awe with open jaws once upon a time and began running on the streets. I felt self-conscious during the initial days in public, thinking I looked silly, too fat or old to run. I'm not able to entirely banish these even now. It is like public speaking. You take time to get comfortable, and sometimes you never will be.

However, I expanded my running experience to marathons, starting from 5k runs to many 10k runs. I broke the myth that you are not too old to start running. Running is an activity dominated by the older generation. Younger runners are impatient and try their best every time, which leads to injuries and setbacks. But older runners are more mature and patient. They enjoy the process, and there are more rewards.

Running won't be easy at first. But it will all be worth it with "runners' high" once you get the hang of it.

I built a professional as well as a runner's community.

From a Kitchen to 'A Corporate Space' at Forty

My hands shook when I arrived at a company office for an interview. For fourteen years, I had been managing a home rather than managing teams. 'Mother' was the sole word on my resume, leaving me with no choice. But sometimes, the scariest beginnings lead to the most beautiful journeys. Looking at myself in the mirror, I remember looking like an imposter in my new formal dress. Parent-teacher meetings were the only networking activity I had.

Later, my perspective shifted as I considered that dealing with a toddler gave me immense patience, which is much needed in the corporate world. My proficiency in tackling household problems could enhance my organizational skills.

Ten pointers for Late Career Starters:

1. Assess Your Skills and Interests.
   Think Outside the Box: Evaluate your professional background and identify any skills that may be relevant to your current occupation.
   Find Transferable Skills: Communication, organization, and time management. These skills are helpful in many jobs.
2. Refresh your Resume and LinkedIn Profile.
   Fill your resume with skills and experience, even from volunteering or personal projects.
   Creating a LinkedIn Profile can be advantageous for connecting with experts in your area and highlighting your abilities.
3. Consider Further Education or Training.
   Engaging in online courses or certifications based on expertise can give you a fresh perspective.
   Workshops: Look for local or community college classes that can help you improve your chances of getting a good job.
4. Network.
   Reach out to old friends and industry acquaintances: Look for opportunities and seek their advice.

Professional groups: Meet people in your area at networking events, webinars or local meetups.

5. Start Small.

   Part-time or freelance work can assist in regaining employment while managing other commitments.

   Having experience through volunteering can enhance your resume and expand your network.

6. Practice Interviewing.

   Prepare for typical interview questions while crafting a narrative about your professional break that emphasizes your readiness to return.

   Carry out a mock interview: Consider conducting an online test.

7. Be Open to Different Opportunities.

   Consider Various Positions: Be willing to explore opportunities that may not meet your criteria but can provide you with valuable skills.

   Temp or Contract Work is a viable option for those seeking flexibility. If desired, they can return to completing their work.

8. Stay Positive and Persistent.

   Despite the difficulty of finding work, remain resilient and maintain a positive attitude.

   Reward yourself: Highlight the small victories you experience when transitioning back into work, such as finishing a program or being interviewed.

9. Take Professional Aid.
   Seek a career coach or counsellor who can offer customized guidance.
10. Set Goals: Set monthly skill goals. Track progress regularly and celebrate small wins.

Essential Reminders:

- Being old is a plus point.
- Every small step counts.
- It is okay to feel overwhelmed.
- Growth takes time.
- Your life experience holds significance.

Upon entering my workplace, my shaking hands have transformed into confident keystrokes. The achievements I never imagined possible have filled my blank resume. While staring at your first job application, realize that the years spent managing homes were not just a career break but a preparation for careers. Your dream isn't torn; it's just waiting for a new pattern. It's natural to feel conflicted about asserting your needs, but you must honour your growth to be the best version of yourself for others.

CHAPTER 5
HEALTH IS WEALTH

Small Steps, Big Gain

I used to take my kids to the lawn tennis when they were in primary school. I had always loved watching people play.

I wondered about the required stamina, agility, reflexes and muscle strength. The coach offered to teach me, along with the kids, in a different group and court. I would have considered the offer had I not been intimidated by the game once when I played with Rajesh on one of our vacations. I also assumed that it would be challenging and double-hard work for a vegetarian woman. The coach tried to convince me that it was not the case. We could always build stamina. Why would I get convinced? I had decided not to, and I also thought he wanted to up the number of people enrolling.

Long ago, I entered the tennis court once at a resort in Panchagani with Rajesh. It looked vast compared to the badminton court. I felt lost, like how we feel lost in the middle of the ocean, and I started gauging how to cover the court. My husband served the ball, and I got terrified as the ball approached me like a missile. I threw the racquet, ducked the ball, and ran out of the court. I never wanted to enter the court again. The experience became a considerable barrier, not even trying another time. Playing tennis without stamina became equivalent to flying an aeroplane for me. Such was the magnitude.

We moved to a new house with a tennis court in the complex. I had already developed a peculiar relationship with the sport, fearing the unknown. However, I fantasized and glamorized it. The blue expanse with white straight patterns from my balcony started attracting me. I yearned to learn the sport and had it in my conversations with people. Once you have built the information over time, you start building confidence. I enrolled in an academy in my neighbourhood. The young coaches were adept at training me. They made efforts to inspire me and push my limits.

Learning the game of lawn tennis has been a challenging and rewarding feat. My challenges were physical and psychological. At first, the idea of being on the court with a racket and some basic skills was startling. Fear of judgment was the first thing I had to deal with.

The other major issue was my fitness status. Tennis requires quickness, stamina, and agility. I had little experience and struggled with the fundamental movements of serving and hitting the ball. Running helps a great deal in any sport. I had run a few marathons, so covering the court was not an issue. I trained only for two months and began practising in the neighbourhood court. But over the months, I slowly built up my fitness with practice. I gradually gained stamina through playing with peers or simply enjoying the game, which helped me overcome my initial challenges.

Ultimately, conquering these obstacles to a certain degree has brought about both tennis skills and lifelong lessons of resilience and determination. Despite the challenges, learning to play lawn tennis still highlights how much perseverance is necessary to overcome life's challenges.

I built a tennis community where each one adds value to the sport.

I'm not a professional player. I do not come any closer to a very skilled player. I play it for fun and to be outdoors in the sun early in the morning.

The struggle to surpass the barrier of self-doubt and low self-confidence can be rewarding, especially when learning new skills like tennis. As a mother of two, I realized that entering the tennis court wasn't solely about playing—I wanted to confront my insecurity and build my self-esteem.

The first time I thought about playing tennis, I felt like a failure and thought it to be for younger people. I had concerns about my age, physical stamina, and ability to compete with younger, more skilled players. I was struggling with self-doubt and a lack of confidence.

I resolved these emotions by establishing achievable targets. I told myself that learning a new skill is sluggish and that everyone who excels was once unsure where to begin. Concentrating on small accomplishments instead of striving for perfection was the key. Every little triumph raised my self-esteem and advanced my confidence in the art. My performance improved, and I became a more assertive woman and mother. By confronting my self-doubt head-on and celebrating my progress, I found that I had the strength to overcome obstacles and pursue my passions, proving that embracing new challenges is never too late for anyone.

I also started improving my yoga poses and tennis. I learnt yoga and meditation when I was thirty-five and saw my body and mind transform.

My Story:

I started by barely being able to run around the block. In yoga, I watched others flow gracefully in all postures while I wriggled with basic poses. Tennis balls would fly past me as I swung inelegantly, but something kept dragging me back to try again.

The first discovery came with accepting my beginnings. I wasn't competing with anyone or my younger self. I was showing up, day after day, building something new.

Ten Actionable Steps for Late-Starting Athletes:

1. Start Where You Are
   - Document your current fitness level
   - Set realistic baseline goals
   - Accept your starting point without judgment

   My truth: I couldn't run 100 meters without stopping

2. Build Basic Strength
   - Begin with simple stretches
   - Practice basic movements
   - Focus on proper form

   Reality: I Started with 10-minute walking, basic yoga stretches

3. Create a Sustainable Schedule
   - Choose consistent time slots
   - Start with 2–3 sessions weekly
   - Allow recovery days

   My approach: Early mornings became my sacred time

4. Handle Physical Limitations
   - Get medical clearance
   - Work with qualified trainers
   - Listen to your body

Learning: Some days were for pushing, others for resting

5. Build Progressive Stamina
   - Increase duration gradually
   - Track improvements weekly
   - Celebrate small victories

   Progress: From walking to running, one minute at a time

6. Master Basic Techniques
   - Learn proper breathing
   - Practice fundamental movements
   - Understand body mechanics

   Journey: From wrong tennis grip to proper form

7. Create Support Systems
   - Join beginners' groups
   - Find workout buddies
   - Share goals with family

   Reality: Found strength in other late starters

8. Handle Age-Related Challenges
   - Focus on flexibility
   - Prioritize recovery
   - Adapt exercises as needed

   Truth: Some poses needed modifications

9. Maintain Motivation
   - Keep a progress journal
   - Take progress photos
   - Set milestone goals

   Success: First 5K completion became possible

10. Build Long-term Habits
    - Create morning routines
    - Plan for obstacles
    - Make exercise non-negotiable

    Achievement: From struggling to regular practice

Essential Reminders:

- Start incredibly small
- Progress beats perfection
- Consistency over intensity
- Recovery is a progress, too
- Age is just a number

Today, I remember that trembling beginner when I served on the tennis court, ran in marathons, or flowed through yoga sequences. Every finish line crossed, every serve achieved, every pose completed started with a straightforward decision - to begin. Your age does not limit your physical dreams; they await your first step.

CHAPTER 6
STEPPING INTO CONFIDENCE: A WALK THAT CHANGED THINGS

"I stare into the gloomy sky. Clouds..... the darkest ones, not so high, approach- to snatch away the light of the beautiful day. I crusade them to pass by.... Alas! They seem as tough as wild rye, never to vanish but multiply. Soon, magic ensues when they untie, squirting rain on my soul that had run dry. Fear of the dark clouds- I let fly at the sky."

I was always a shy, underconfident child. As a young girl, I used to reflect critically, focusing on imperfections and exaggerating the negative aspects of my appearance. Family, peers, or others during formative years can significantly affect self-esteem.

Why are women sensitive to minor insults but never believe a positive one? Criticisms are stored forever. Compliments fade quickly. "I can't even go in for the brief skirt", "These pants make me look like a potato". These are the self-talk we get to hear. After watching Pretty Woman, I discovered that a lot of us share the same level of self-doubt, which caused Julia Roberts' character to be derailed. In a scene, she confides in entrepreneur Richard Gere that no one wants to work as a sex worker and that her motivation for it was her lack of self-assertion. Gere acknowledges that she possesses immense potential and skill. She replies, "It's easy to believe the bad stuff".

The surge of hormones in a woman's brain makes her more sensitive to emotional nuances like disapproval and rejection. How you interpret feedback from others depends on where you are in your cycle. "Some days that feedback will boost your confidence, and other days it'll knock you down".

Since childhood, I have been fascinated by walking on the ramp. It was not just the glamour and the lights that captivated me when I saw women walking on the ramp; it was the confidence that captivated me.

It all started when I saw a flyer from a resident in the society's WhatsApp group. It was a walk for a mother and her child. As my kids were not keen to walk, I planned to do it alone. I was a working woman, and my days used to be tight with work, kids, and household chores. I just wanted to walk and experience it and never focused on winning it. I had not prepared well for the introduction round. We had a day's workshop, where I learned about posture, expressions, and walking. I experienced a surge of excitement as I learned to embrace my body. I was free of the results that day as I was not keen on winning.

Walking in heels and walking down the runway gave me a boost of confidence. I enjoyed the whole event being myself. It taught me the value of being present and that stepping out of my comfort zone could lead to amazing things.

Surprisingly, I won first runner-up. I came home with a small crown sash (a silk strap around one shoulder where the title is written). It was the day when my critical inner voice mellowed down, gave me hope, and introduced me to the newer me.

I got promoted on the professional front. It called for shift changes and working from home the entire night to match the US time. My health took a toll, and my daughter's board exams approached. I couldn't pull it off for a long. I had to resign, and I did. After fourteen years of hiatus, I credit Amazon for giving wings to my flight. It was where I started building something for myself and going beyond the realms of the house and my family. It planted the seed of freedom, endless possibilities, and confidence in my life. I was ready to slow down and explore life more.

After a year, I won a subtitle in the Mrs India sports category and later was crowned as a winner of Mrs. Swag Icon of India, a task-based contest.

Many people think it's all about big hair, beauty, walking around on stage, and plastic. It has more to it. There are many positive aspects one gains through these daunting preparation and presentation processes during the pageant:

- Builds one's confidence: Among the millions of reasons to enter a beauty pageant, the most important is building trust in oneself
- Lessons one learns: You will learn many things, not just about yourself but about communication skills, leadership, interviewing, attitude, and more. Beauty pageants are an entry point for anyone who wants to be on stage, give back, and learn more about themselves.
- Friendship/Family: Despite the clichés of mean girl fights and fake artificial personalities, the girls you compete with become your family. You will be glad to know that cliches are not valid.
- Opportunities: Beauty pageants bring you many opportunities. It gives a platform to express yourself
- Community Involvement: The best part of any glamorous event is collaborating or setting up an organization.

- The Crown: Of course, the crown and sash are practically the highlight of the competition. The title itself! But someone once told me, "The crown does not define you; you define the crown. In other words, you make the crown, so do something good, something great and make a difference".
- The New You: I would never back out of any competition I've ever participated in. I am grateful for every experience I have had. I may not have won them all, but I have taken home more than just crowns and titles.

The pageants present an idealized representation of femininity and grace. They can provide more than just a glamorous appearance. The contests taught me some important life lessons about myself that I had not been aware of.

Developing strong self-assurance and awareness is crucial in preparing for competition. I confronted my insecurities by practising public speaking, poise and grace, and overcoming stage fright. My presence on stage spoke about my inner strength and determination. This expedition taught me that confidence wasn't just about looks but about accepting and believing in yourself.

I realized my passion for advocating social responsibility. The combination of community service projects and statements during competition fuelled my desire to make a difference in the world. Participating in outreach programs made me realize the power of my voice to bring about change. I understood that beauty does not depend solely on appearance; it also involves character and the ability to inspire others.

Besides, pageants' competitiveness fostered courage. Facing rejection or not achieving the desired outcome can be disheartening, but these situations give rise to resilience and the capacity to persevere. I learned that setbacks are not failures but stepping stones toward personal growth.

Contests function as a mirror, unveiling truths about self-confidence, social responsibility, and resilience. They told me to accept myself and strive for betterment. Finally, the experience showed that true beauty is in the strength, service, and courage to be genuine.

****

"Crowning Your Worth"

At 44, I found myself staring at an advertisement for a beauty pageant. My first thought was laughter: Who would enter a beauty pageant at my age? My second thought was horror. But somewhere deep inside, a long-buried dream stirred.

My Journey Through Reality:

Walking in heels after years in comfortable flats, learning to pose when my body felt foreign, practising public speaking when my voice shook - every step challenged my skills and self-image.

Ten Real Steps for Pageant Aspirants of my age:

1. Face Your True Reflection
   My experience:
   - Taking a critical look at myself for the first time in years
   - Recognizing my apologetic attitude
   - I realized that I had forgotten how to walk upright

   Reality check: It started with just standing upright for 5 minutes

2. Building Basic Confidence
   - Practiced walking in high heels at home
   - Recorded my voice to improve the tone
   - Learned a basic skincare routine

   Truth: It took countless attempts to walk smoothly again

3. Dealing with Age Concerns (Actual Challenges):
   - Competing with younger contestants
   - Dealing with physical changes
   - Dealing with family reactions

   Solution: Turned age into a story of strength

4. Creating a Platform(My Approach):
   - Listed my life experiences
   - Understood what I stand for
   - Developed authentic answers

   Reality: My motherhood gave me a unique perspective

5. Physical Preparation (Practical Steps):
   - Starting a basic fitness routine
   - learning makeup techniques
   - Gradually improving posture

   The journey: From casual posture to stage presence

6. Mental Conditioning (Daily Practices):
   - Practicing positive self-talk
   - Visualization techniques
   - Confidence-boosting activities

   Truth: I cried after my first practice session

7. Skill Development
   - Public Speaking Practice
   - Stage Presence Training
   - Interview Preparation

   Progress: From Trembling Voice to Clear Speech

8. Image Building
   - Wardrobe Assessment
   - Personal Style Development
   - Learning Courtesy and Etiquette

   Challenge: Finding Age-Appropriate Attractiveness

9. Contest Preparation (Actual Process):
   - Interviews
   - Runway Practice
   - Speech Rehearsals

   Reality: Practicing in the living room after the kids are in bed
10. Authenticity (Core Focus):
    - Staying true to your story
    - Use your life experiences
    - Embrace your uniqueness

    Success: At my age, I could make it because of authenticity

Essential Truths:

- Age adds depth to your story
- Experience is your crown
- Authenticity beats perfection
- It's never too late to shine

When I stood on stage at 44 and wore my crown for the first time, I realized the journey wasn't just about earning a title. It was about crowning the woman who had been hiding behind roles and responsibilities. For all the women who think they are "too old", – pageants aren't about perfect beauty; they're about perfectly embracing who you are.

CHAPTER 7
GIVING BACK: PURPOSE THROUGH SERVICE

One of the tasks in a pageant was to pack ten boxes of food, set out on the streets, and feed those in need once every week. I did that, and I felt complete that day. I had felt slight discomfort for years and could not pinpoint at one point. I recognized what it was about- the day I gave food without planning.

Discomfort is often the first step to recognizing that you need to do more or something different. For me, a constant feeling that I could do more to improve the situation of others marked my discomfort.

At first, I felt inadequate and insecure. My question was, "Can I make a difference"? Understanding that change can only come in small steps, I decided to find a way to make a difference.

I started visiting a local school for the underprivileged. I decided to impart English communication skills and moral learning to students.

Teaching English and Moral Education to the kids was one of my most rewarding experiences. It was exciting. Even though they came from various backgrounds and experienced many challenges, the children showed unwavering dedication to learning.

Despite their lack of proficiency in communicating effectively in English, the students' determination to improve was inspiring. Through engaging activities like games, storytelling, and role-playing, I improved their language skills and made learning more enjoyable. Witnessing their growth and development was a delight.

The inclusion of moral education in the curriculum was equally crucial. In my presentation, I emphasized the importance of moral values like honesty, respect, and kindness while discussing practical applications of these values. Additionally, the children were enthusiastic participants in these discussions, sharing their stories and providing insights into their daily lives.

I learned that teaching is a two-way process. I aimed to impart knowledge, but at the same time, I also learned valuable lessons from the children about the power of resilience and hope. The students' laughter and enthusiasm brightened up the classroom, highlighting that education is not solely about academic achievement but also about cultivating positive qualities and building character. I did this for more than a year and have taken a break since some moths and intend to resume shortly.

I also joined the Robinhood Army, which serves food to needy people. Recently, I initiated the Robinhood Academy in my neighbourhood. We scouted for a cluster of kids who needed mentorship. Establishing Robinhood Academy in my locality was crucial to bettering the youth and creating an environment conducive to learning. It aims to provide young students with free educational resources, mentorship, tutoring and educational support. The goal is to provide a nurturing environment where students can succeed academically and socially with the assistance of enthusiastic volunteers.

The first step in launching the academy was gathering young volunteers from the local community who were enthusiastic about education and mentoring. The main focus was cultivating a strong sense of community among the volunteers and encouraging them to contribute by making alterations.

We assist students of all levels in math and English. In addition, life skills, career guidance, and personal growth mentorship would help students prepare for the real world beyond their studies. Mentoring volunteers with their expertise enhances the learning process and fosters a sense of authenticity, which can benefit mentor/mentee relationships.

In addition to academic support, Robinhood Academy would emphasize creating a positive community atmosphere. Organizing regular events, such as community cleanups or sports days, would engage families and neighbourhood residents, fostering a collective spirit of support and collaboration.

My understanding of giving has deepened over time.

Giving back to others has rewarded me with personal growth and self-awareness. Through various service activities, I have learned much about myself and my values and discovered that helping others is a fundamental aspect of my personality.

Through my involvement in the community, volunteering at local shelters, and participating in environmental cleanups, I have discovered the ability to empathize and connect with people from different backgrounds. It has taught me the importance of kindness and understanding and strengthened my belief that we all share a common humanity. Each interaction has given me a unique insight into the struggles and triumphs of others and often caused me to reflect more deeply on my own life.

Furthermore, giving back has helped me recognize my passions and strengths. For example, I thrive in a supportive environment where I can contribute ideas and support others. This recognition boosted my confidence and encouraged me to seek opportunities to lead and inspire rather than exist in the background. It is so gratifying to see that my efforts can make a visible difference in someone's life and foster a sense of purpose within myself.

I have also learned the importance of humility. Giving back is not about self-promotion or validation but about generosity and helpfulness. I value opportunities to make a positive impact in the lives of others while remaining firmly grateful for what I have.

In summary, giving back has revealed my values, strengths, and the true essence of my character. The experience has instilled in me a deep appreciation for the interconnectedness of our lives and the power of altruism, ultimately making me a more compassionate and confident person.

I use social platforms to advocate for issues I care about, whether through social media, speaking, or writing. I raise awareness, share personal experiences, encourage dialogue, and influence public opinion to spur meaningful debate on important issues. Advocacy can bring attention to underrepresented voices, challenge social norms, and mobilize communities for collective action.

Ten Actionable Steps for Service Leadership:

1. Start Small but Significant
   - Begin with your immediate community
   - Identify one local need you can address
   - Use existing skills to help others

   Example: Started with teaching basic English to neighbourhood helpers

2. Build on Personal Experience
   - List your life lessons
   - Identify who could benefit
   - Create simple sharing methods

   Reality: I used my late-career start to mentor other women

3. Create Sustainable Impact
   - Choose causes you can commit to long-term
   - Build reliable support systems
   - Develop repeatable programs

   Progress: weekly mentorship for young children

4. Leverage Your Network
   - Connect with like-minded individuals
   - Build community partnerships
   - Share resources and knowledge

   Truth: It started with one school and expanded to another cluster.

5. Measure Real Impact
   - Track the progress of beneficiaries
   - Document success stories

- Gather feedback for improvement

Achievement: Helping young children build confidence in English communication.

6. Handle Challenges
   - Balance time commitments
   - Manage limited resources
   - Deal with resistance

   Solution: Create structured programs with clear boundaries

7. Scale Thoughtfully
   - Expand based on capacity
   - Train other leaders
   - Document processes

   Growth: From one community to another neighbourhood

8. Maintain Momentum
   - Set regular service schedules
   - Create accountability systems
   - Celebrate small victories

   Reality: Monthly goals keep us focused

9. Build Leadership
   - Identify potential leaders
   - Share responsibilities
   - Create succession plans

   Development: Working with many community leaders as volunteers

10. Ensure Sustainability
    - Create resource banks
    - Document best practices
    - Build support networks

    Legacy: Self-sustaining community programs

Essential Learning:

- Service heals the server
- Impact matters more than scale
- Consistency beats intensity
- Community builds strength

CHAPTER 8
FINDING MY VOICE

"She mines the hidden pieces of her being. They gush through every vein of her body and bring her alive to a grand show called art".

*I*t would sound slightly different, but I'm speaking from my writing experience. I was not an avid reader, but I have written in magazines and local newspapers, co-authored two books, compiled one, and edited two. Writing is a gift/talent like singing or dancing and a skill one can develop.

The power of writing has always been a tool for people to express their ideas, feelings, and experiences. While some people start this journey in their youth, it was when I reached adulthood that I truly understood the transformative power of poetry. I found it hard to control my emotions and sometimes felt overwhelmed.

Writing poems helped me understand my thoughts and how I processed them. Poetry changed my life by helping me express my feelings and share my thoughts, allowing me to connect to myself. Each poem captures different emotions, including happiness, sadness, loss, or yearning.

The act of creating a creative solution to my emotional turmoil is both comforting and healing. My first published work was a poem for the college magazine during my graduation years.

Before getting married, I was unfamiliar with reading fat books or novels. For a long time, I had no idea how people found pleasure in reading lengthy narratives and how they managed to do so. I often marvelled at people who could stomach and had the patience to sit with a fat book.

I enjoyed the colourful layout and small, compact pieces. Comics offered amusement and a unique combination of art and story. The joy they provided was derived from swift humour and captivating illustrations, demonstrating that literature could exist in various forms and did not always have to be lengthy.

After I got married, things changed slightly. I started reading fat books; at least I could finish some. I had never been able to appreciate the beauty of intricate plots, characters, and emotions until I read novels. I was immersed in different worlds each time I read new books, allowing myself to live as one of the characters and explore intricate themes. Having said this, reading novels and other nonfiction was far and wide.

In 2017, I started a blog as one of the projects in the course I had enrolled in. I wanted to fill the blog, so I wrote more poems and tried writing short stories, fiction and nonfiction. Some of my friends liked them. My blog is a basic one with less content. However, it gave me some push to write stories.

Community

By joining a writing community and participating in online forums, I have improved in writing in various forms. Writing can be a lonely place. Feedback from other writers helps me refine my writing style and enhance my narratives. I am exposed to different writing styles and genres as I work alongside diverse voices in a broader context, expanding my knowledge of what's possible within the craft.

The writing community provides a supportive environment where members support each other through the challenges and ups of their writing journey. This sense of togetherness has given me the strength to embrace change and accept rejection and criticism as opportunities for growth rather than facing setbacks.

Authoring

Later, I was invited to contribute to an anthology that included short stories and poems. I submitted my work. The same publication allowed me to compile a book on the anthology of short stories. I had the freedom to choose the theme, genre, and authors. I contacted people in my network and could rope in around twelve writers. I co-authored, compiled and edited the book. Holding the book was a magical experience. The physical copy of the book evoked feelings of pride in me. It was a tangible manifestation of my dedication and many gifted individuals' efforts.

Writing this book was a profound and informative experience. By incorporating the input of multiple writers and enhancing their concepts into cohesive tales, I gained a deeper understanding of collaboration. Each step in the process contributed to my learning. The thrill of merging voices with a common theme made every late-night editing worth it. Each writer contributed a unique perspective, creating layered and varied ideas that made up our collective mind.

As I read it, I felt a sense of pride. It was surreal to see the printed words culminating in our efforts. I recollected the brainstorming sessions, revisions, and meticulously selected items to ensure matching. It went beyond stories; it became a testament to the power of community and shared vision.

I felt the book in my hands, returning memories of the bonds that made this experience possible. Each writer demonstrated dedication and passion through writing.

The effort was driven by mutual respect and admiration, demonstrating the potential of working together towards a common goal.

Editing

One of the authors of the book I compiled wanted me to edit his solo book of short stories. I agreed, and it was not a mean feat. I sat for nearly six hours a day for almost three months.

Editing a book requires creativity and organization skills. An anthology of literature is a collection of written works categorized into different genres, themes, or voices, each representing varying aspects related to corresponding topics or lives. My role was to curate these pieces carefully.

The curation process was challenging and enjoyable, enabling a dynamic exchange of ideas.

I proceeded to edit the pieces after determining their appropriateness, clarity, and overall flow. I had to work closely with the author, keeping in mind that his voice was unique and contributing to an overall improvement of the writing.

Editing anthologies is arduous and demands fervour and skill. At its core, it celebrates and promotes diversity of thought, making literature accessible to more readers.

Turning myself into a book author was like a turning point where I discovered who I was and what I already knew. Reading whole books was once daunting, and I struggled to get through them. However, I began exploring different styles and perspectives over the years. The process sparked a surge of introspection—an essential component of my evolution.

I began to understand the meaning behind each book as it impacted me, even as I read them. Reading was not just a way to understand; it was primarily based on empathy and connection, as I learned. I started interacting with characters, their struggles, and triumphs, making me reflect on my experiences.

A change in attitude was the key to my evolution. I did not consider reading a task, but the transition motivated me to take shelter in pen and paper to convert my ideas into written words. Each setback I experienced was a source of strength and encouragement, teaching me to embrace the unknown and move forward with determination.

Becoming an author was about crafting a book and embracing vulnerability. I could create stories that resonated with others, connecting the dots between my experiences and those of others.

Manifesting the Torn Dream and Expressing My Truth Through Writing

When it comes to expressing our desires and aspirations, writing is about exploring the depth of our identity. If someone has a torn dream—an old or new one—it's essential to view this loss as an opportunity for progress. Addressing the torn dream can help one find one's true self and gain insight.

Identifying the emotions associated with the conflicted dream is crucial. Although many people may feel disappointed or lost, the feelings can be utilized to uncover their identity. Recuperation begins with the question of what that dream once meant.

Ten ways in which you can use writing to rebuild yourself and find your voice:

1. Reflect: Reflect on your ripped dream, what it meant for you then and how it made you feel.
2. Journal: Write down your daily experiences, emotions, and aspirations in a journal to clarify your thoughts.
3. Set your intentions: what do you want to achieve through your writing? Knowing your purpose will shape the way you present yourself.
4. Read widely: Read extensively to refine your writing style and expand your understanding.

5. Authenticity: Be free to express your thoughts without fear. Authenticity resonates with readers.
6. Request Feedback: Discuss your work with trusted associates or instructors to gain knowledge and insight.
7. Explore your creativity: Try different writing styles, such as poetry, essays, or stories, to find what resonates with you.
8. Engage in a Writing Guild: Joining forces with peers can provide encouragement and support while creating an ambience for open dialogue.
9. Consider the importance of self-compassion in writing about brutal truths. Don't be rude to yourself.
10. Be Dedicated: Writing is a lifetime experience. Stay committed to your practice and allow it to develop alongside you.

When individuals write down their torn dreams and find inner peace in writing, they can use it to turn their pain into compelling stories that resonate with others.

CHAPTER 9
LOSS OF AN ANCHOR AND LIFE-LONG LEARNING

I was already working and having a voice at the grassroots level, so I was appointed State President of the Women's Indian Chamber of Commerce and Industry, Maharashtra (WICCI). It is a leading national women's business chamber with a bold vision to create a global impact for entrepreneurs, businesswomen, and professionals from all walks of life. We promote and build women's entrepreneurship and business by strengthening our engagement with governments, institutions, global trade, and networks.

Upskilling yourself is essential in this age, as things relevant five years ago are redundant in some years. I enrolled in a one-year data science course at IIT Roorkee. It went on so well. I was elated to learn new technology, and I love the subjects. During the course and my recent visit to the IIT Roorkee campus, I interacted with experienced industry training experts and IIT professors. I exchanged ideas and thoughts with students from various colleges.

It's often said that tech is a hard place for women, but many elements of the tech industry make it ideal for women in many ways. The industry's flexibility differs from what I've experienced in other sectors. In many tech companies, it's widely accepted that people can work from anywhere on their schedule. It makes a massive difference if you want a career and a family. Additionally, the tech industry is often very meritocratic, with results judged based on quantifiable results (products launched, products sold, figures achieved, etc.). This is also helpful for women, as it removes some subjective judgments that women may face professionally.

The most critical advice for girls and women considering a tech career is the same for all women and girls worldwide: the most important thing is to believe in your abilities. Women often underestimate their abilities, preventing them from taking on challenges that allow them to reach their potential. Stereotype threat – the phenomenon in which people are more likely to act on stereotypes when they are aware of them – is a serious problem for girls studying science, math, and technology. Girls don't do it because they don't believe they can be good at it. (This is why girls often do better in these subjects in all-girls schools.) If women thought they could succeed in tech, they would. And so many great tech leaders are already doing this.

Loss of an anchor

After my mom passed away in 2016, my dad had been a strong anchor for me till his death in November 2023. I was in the middle of the IIT course. It would take a lifetime to match up to his passion, courage, bravery, and sophistication. He had an aura that no one could match. My mother has poured giving, kindness and love into my life. She was a giver and epitome of compassion and patience. Whatever I do in life would be for them, an ode to them to carry their legacy.

I dealt with the loss by talking about it: Talking about the death and life of a loved one can help you understand and process the loss.

Acknowledging the emotions: Many emotions naturally arise during the grieving process. The best thing you can do is recognise these emotions and allow them to come and go.

Celebrating a loved one's life can take many forms. In memory of my loved ones, I gave more, worked harder, and brought positivity. Losing my parents has reinforced the reality of our impermanence and insignificance.

Helping others: A change in identity—going from being somebody's child to being the older generation—has made me more aware of my responsibilities inside and outside the family.

Ten Tips for Women in Technology Realm:

1. Keep learning
   Learning and developing in areas where you are not confident is essential. Courses or training can help you fill your skills and knowledge gaps.
2. Networking
   Both professional and personal networking help. Keep your LinkedIn page updated and engage with the people.
3. Share about your success
   Your success and career progress often go unnoticed by yourself and those around you. From time to time, it's good to reflect on how far you've come. Many universities, schools and career sites offer case studies on their alums or people in related industries.
4. You are not alone – mentoring helps
   By becoming a mentor, you can pass on valuable knowledge and experience to others looking to learn and progress in a similar industry. This is a great way to get recognised by your employers and colleagues, and you'll also get a sense of self-accomplishment because it feels great to help others. Alternatively,

finding another woman in the tech industry to mentor you is a great way to advance your career and knowledge. You'll gain more experience than college would, as your mentor will work in real-life scenarios and be able to impart their wealth of education. Participating in a mentorship program will show you are willing to learn, which is very attractive to potential employers.

5. Feedback helps you grow and criticism is a positive sign

   You need to see criticism as an opportunity, not a negative one. Feedback is the first step for improvement.

6. Say No to Burn Out

   Physical and mental Burnout is a serious issue for tech women. Discuss concerns with your manager and prioritise. Self-care through hobbies, family time, and exercise.

7. Attend Industry Events

   Industry events enhance your understanding of your field and keep you updated.

8. Communicate with Your Colleagues and Boss

   Regular communication is crucial for team productivity. Communicate with the boss and team members for your healthy growth.

9. Set Personal Goals

   Setting personal goals with a timeline can motivate you and guide your career growth.

10. Immerse Yourself in the Tech Industry
   Follow relevant social media accounts to keep up with the latest news, trends, and influential technological figures, aiding you in learning continuously.

In my recent interview with the COEP blog team, I addressed and explored key topics like feminism, patriarchy, and women's empowerment. The discussion shed light on women's challenges and the importance of gender equality in workplaces and today's world. I have placed the importance of community and support, which one needs to build to grow.

I have built a community in every field I have entered, which has proved to be a game changer in empowering me. This is more important to homemakers. Being a housewife is lonely without much exposure to the outer world. Trying to have different experiences and endeavours not only builds your confidence, exposure, and communities, but it also makes you. You explore more about yourself while exploring the world outside. The growth will be inside out. So, gal, start today. It is never too late.

CHAPTER 10
STITCHING THE TAPESTRY OF MY LIFE

"The chapters of Life, one ends, the new one arises. I grudge about the disconnects. I whack and look behind. I then, comprehend it to be a perfect read woven by a thread chapter after chapter"

Self-discovery

Understanding oneself is a profound journey often comprised of various experiences and endeavours. Our lives are intertwined, leading to a more profound sense of self that emerges in each phase as we age. People can explore their personalities, strengths, and weaknesses by engaging in various personal, educational, or professional activities.

Whenever we venture outside our comfort zone, we encounter new things that provide insight and change us about ourselves. Playing sports as a team can reveal one's leadership or team spirit; while exploring art, one may find another hidden talent. Our experiences enhance our skill set, which also aids in comprehending our emotional responses, preferences, and values. These endeavours are interconnected. An issue in one area may impact another; the resilience acquired during a sporting event could also enhance academic performance. The lessons we gain from every experience profoundly influence our moves and judgments. Developing patience while learning a musical instrument can improve one's aptitude for managing intricate tasks at work.

This process needs reflection. Looking back and recognizing past events' significance can help establish meaningful connections between different pursuits. The understanding can facilitate a more profound sense of self-worth, leading to choices that align with one's values and aspirations.

In conclusion, knowing oneself through many experiences creates a rich tapestry of self-discovery. Each endeavour serves as a stepping stone, enhancing our understanding of personal identity and fostering growth. Ultimately, the interrelated nature of these experiences encourages a holistic view of oneself, promoting lifelong learning and self-improvement.

Self-discovery is an ongoing process. It evolves as we navigate through different life stages and challenges. Embracing change and remaining open to new experiences are essential to this journey. By committing to self-discovery, individuals can achieve a more authentic and fulfilling life marked by self-awareness, resilience, and a profound connection to their true selves. In conclusion, self-discovery is an invaluable journey that shapes our identities and enriches our lives.

Self-Love

Self-love is welcoming your uniqueness and counting yourself to walk your path confidently. It means working unashamedly to achieve your wildest dreams. It means working now so you won't look back in the future with regrets. It's important to give yourself the time and space to define what self-love means in your life outside of superficial wellness routines like manicures and solo dates. I like to pamper myself as much as others, but self-love is about finding the courage to dig deep inside and get into the most unclear parts of my relationship with myself. It means being comfortable with my darker side, listening to my mind, body and soul, and nourishing myself accordingly.

It took time, but I realized that I was trying to fix something that wasn't broken. I always wanted to do more meaningful things, and I wanted to dedicate myself, my passion, and my focus to everything I did. As a whole person and a healed person, I know that self-love means valuing myself enough to let go of the things that don't particularly value me without regret. The areas I ventured into were about discipline. Being disciplined in one area of my life helped me to discipline other things, like my emotions and the people I let into my space. I gained clarity and was able to focus only on ME. That's when I began to learn to love ME truly.

Points to remember to achieve Perfect Self-Love

Even when you're not feeling powerful, remind yourself how far you've come and how you've survived. You are here now, alive and more vigorous than ever imagined. Be patient with yourself.

1. Stop comparing yourself to others.
   We are raised to be competitive, so comparing yourself to others is natural. But that can be dangerous. There is only one you in the world, so there is no point in comparing yourself to anyone else. Instead, focus on yourself and your journey. The shift in energy alone will set you free.
2. Don't worry about what others think.
   Similarly, don't worry about what society thinks or expects of you. You can't please everyone. It is a waste of your time and energy and hinders your growth.
3. Allow yourself to make mistakes.
   We've been told since we were tiny that "no one is perfect; everyone makes mistakes", and as we get older, we start to feel pressured never to fail. Don't

be so hard on yourself! Allow yourself to fail and fall to learn and grow from them. Embrace your past. You are constantly changing, evolving from who you were to who you are today and who you will become.

So, forget the voice in your head telling you must be perfect. The lessons you can learn from mistakes are invaluable.

4. Remember that your worth does not depend on your body's appearance.

   It is fundamental! So many things try to distract you from this powerful truth. In some cases, even your own internalized sexism can reinforce the idea that you are not enough. You are worthwhile because of who you are, not your body. So, wear what makes you feel good, happy, comfortable and confident.

5. Don't be afraid to let go of toxic people.

   Not everyone can take responsibility for the energy they put into the world. If people are bringing toxicity and not taking responsibility, you may need to let go of them. Don't be afraid. It's liberating and vital, even if it's painful.

   Remember: Guard your energy. Removing yourself from situations or people that drain your energy is not rude or wrong.

6. Dealing with fear.

    Fear, like mistakes, is natural and human. Don't deny your fear; understand it. This healthy exercise is highly beneficial for your mental health. Questioning and evaluating your worries can help you gain clarity and uncover the issues in your life that are causing the anxiety.

7. Trust that you are making a good decision for yourself.

    We often doubt ourselves and our ability to do the right thing, even though we know what is best in our hearts. Remember that your feelings are valid; they are not blind to reality. You know yourself better than anyone, so be your most prominent advocate.

8. Take advantage of every opportunity, or create your own.

    The timing for your next big step in life is never perfect. The conditions may not be ideal, but don't let that stop you from achieving your goals and dreams. Instead, seize the moment because it may never come again.

9. Put yourself first.

    Don't feel bad. Women, mainly, may be used to putting others first. There is a time and a place for this, but it shouldn't be a habit that damages your mental or emotional health.

Take it easy. If you don't relax and refuel, you can take a lot out of yourself. Whether that means spending the day in bed or outdoors in nature, find something that relaxes you and make time for it.

10. Feel the pain and pleasure as intensely as possible.
    Feel things intensely. Get involved in the pain, indulge in the pleasure, and don't put limits on your emotions. Fear, pain, and joy can help you understand yourself and ultimately realize that you are not your emotions.

11. Be courageous in public.
    Get into the habit of speaking your mind. Courage is like a muscle; the more you exercise it, the stronger it will grow. Don't wait for permission to sit at the table. Join the conversation. Post your thoughts. Know that your voice is as important as others.'

12. Find beauty in small things.
    Try noticing at least one beautiful, small thing around you daily. Write it down and be grateful for it. Gratitude not only gives you a new perspective, it is also essential for finding joy.

13. Be kind to yourself.
    The world has harsh words and criticism—don't mix your own. Speak kindly to yourself and avoid saying mean things. You've come so far and grown so much. Don't forget to celebrate yourself, and not just on your birthday.

Takeaway

Self-love and self-discovery don't happen overnight. But over time, it will take root in your heart.

You may struggle, but looking back at these moments, you will see they were stepping stones to becoming your best self.

Summary

Awakening to a New Chapter:

Story:

Once upon a time, a young girl named Elara lived in a quaint village between the mountains. She was known for her cheerful disposition and kind heart, but deep down, she felt a void. One day, she stumbled upon an ancient, weathered book in the village library titled "The Journey to Self". Intrigued, Elara decided to take it home.

As she flipped through the yellowed pages, she found a map that led to various landmarks representing different aspects of oneself: the Valley of Dreams, the Forest of Fears, and the Mountain of Strength. With a spark of curiosity igniting within her, Elara set off on her journey.

First, she ventured into the Valley of Dreams, where she discovered her aspirations and hopes. Here, she met a wise older man who reminded her that dreams are the blueprints of one's future. Elara realized she had always wanted to be an artist but had buried that dream beneath her daily responsibilities.

Next, she braved the Forest of Fears, where treacherous shadows whispered her insecurities. Each bush and tree symbolized her fear, such as failure and rejection. She faced them one by one with courage, understanding that fears could either bind or propel her forward. By the time she emerged, she felt lighter, freed from the chains of doubt.

The final destination was the Mountain of Strength. Here, Elara reflected on her challenges and hardships. She learned that every struggle had built her resilience and character and that embracing these lessons was key to knowing herself.

Returning home, Elara felt whole. The journey taught her that knowing oneself is a lifelong adventure. She became an artist, using her experiences to inspire others to share her story of self-discovery with the world.

***

Embark on the transformative journey of stitching together your fragmented dreams using the vibrant and uplifting threads of self-discovery and self-love. Each thread represents a lesson learned, a moment of growth, or a realization about your true self. As you weave these elements into an intricate tapestry, you will create a vivid representation of your life. This masterpiece reflects your challenges and triumphs and your unique essence. It is crucial to understand that this enriching process is one that only you can navigate; you hold the key to crafting your narrative.

"I'm not waiting for someone to stitch my torn dreams, to mend my bruised heart that aches with every beat, to light up the dark abyss that gapes from right down my feet. Shadows and I coexist making me fierce and great I'm not waiting to be 'Perfect'"

---

www.ingramcontent.com/pod-product-compliance
Lightning Source LLC
LaVergne TN
LVHW041537070526
838199LV00046B/1705